BRIGHT BRAVE PHENOMENA

BRIGHT BRAVE PHENOMENA

POEMS

Amanda Nadelberg

COFFEE HOUSE PRESS

MINNEAPOLIS

2012

Coffee House Press books are available to the trade through our primary distributor, Consortium Book Sales & Distribution, www.cbsd.com or (800) 283-3572. For personal orders, catalogs, or other information, write to: info@coffeehousepress.org.

Coffee House Press is a nonprofit literary publishing house. Support from private foundations, corporate giving programs, government programs, and generous individuals helps make the publication of our books possible. We gratefully acknowledge their support in detail in the back of this book. To you and our many readers around the world, we send our thanks for your continuing support.

Good books are brewing at coffeehousepress.org

LIBRARY OF CONGRESS CATALOGING-IN-PUBLICATION DATA
Nadelberg, Amanda.
Bright brave phenomena : poems / by Amanda Nadelberg.
p. cm.
ISBN 978-1-56689-303-9 (alk. paper)
I. Title.
PS3614.A28B75 2012
811'.6—DC23
2011029251

Printed in the United States
3 5 7 9 8 6 4

CREDITS
In "Powerage" the phrase "*bite me you big-balled boogie man*" is borrowed from C.D. Wright's *Deepstep Come Shining*.

The title "You Were Shoveling Snow and I Was the Snow" is borrowed from the film *The Family Stone*.

Some poems in this book are written after Éric Rohmer's *Six Moral Tales* and *Comedies and Proverbs*.

Absence is to love what the wind is to fire. When it's a small fire, the wind kills it. But when it's a real fire, it intensifies it. So the absence should do that.

—DIANE VON FURSTENBERG

I am the little departing song
and just like that there's this.
One more time, a house isn't a house
but a home, how a body and a body just
happen. Lying in the false woods of
a room, faces go empty—empty reason,
a non-broken man—these bright brave
phenomena like complete reverie. The
bride and groom were shivering, it
actually started to snow. The shadow
of the mind stood up, changed tables,
like a plane I was coming and going.
Furniture happening places it shouldn't,
blank bodies on the wrong half of the
world, we don't know what to do. The lake
and fields quiet broken for winter
but you are still worth thinking, and so
in the tiny century of my mouth
I see you sitting in a window holding
forth, charming the backpacks right
into the night. There were no thoughts
before feet appeared, there was no
time for mapping. The floor of the river

answered the phone, took a message—
the fire smelled of peanuts, the telephone
like stars—it was forever ago dear friend,
you beast, and still I won't let go.

MARKET RUIN

In the flowers we slept over
ourselves. Remarkable
went home, quiet as it could,
the brighter forest, our bad sleep
habits. I don't remember who
quit first but I was tired and
you asked all the wrong questions.
Porches carrying anything,
I want more than that. What
happens to the body is delicate,
a secret holding a dress absolute,
and you're the river, putting
dragon in my shoe. Everyone
loves fire, la, la!, some are
sleeping and these things
happen—some departments

feign broken, deal with it.
If everyone had sounds
they'd be willing to make
then patience might let us
let the sky stop working when

we looked to the east sometimes. Imagine
the beautiful mistake. We all know
how the farm got there and how it
managed to stay, I'm not about
to lecture you on anything, I've
got my own problems. Thoughts
of an unmoving violence, the river
terrible still, it's not that they
are not sensitive, it's just, I think,
they're broken. I heard rain, it
wasn't raining, I couldn't close my eyes.

And when I looked out

the big windows and you

were there too and all

there was to see was elephants

and angry elephants at

that. Their trunks

halving bodies as they

threw with their mouths.

And there was you and me

in a window room

watching it, me

totally for you. Light

lipped. I couldn't

say a thing. Even if

you can never love me. That

day the elephants took

over the world. You gave me

a terrible hug and you

kissed me on the eyebrow.

The wonderment of hysteria!

The generosity of your fear!

The open mouth moves to the field,

uncovers lost teeth and little white

birds taking notes on talking.

In this way and barely, the grass moves

with intention. Strong indications

of the mouth, I will still shower,

which is good. The maps now stuck

in the tallest grass, you will stay

until everything's over. Having beat

the rain, the country is different

for absence. Sympathetic ass, you

will wait. Without any edges the light

is slow, without teeth, never mind. It is

just too bad. Waking children from

anything, the sun keeps going and our

people go back to the supposed farm.

Nature abhors a vacuum, and I say things

because I'm going to lead you to a place and

when we get there it will be so sad. Like you won't

be able to find your feet, and we are small

animals. We could have that in common,

if you'd try being kind. We are a lot of

clapping here. So you don't like flowers?

Fine. Hideous people can have each other,

I don't care. I just don't want to be

the assassin. It would kill the mice.

POWERAGE

after AC/DC

i.

The beets are done
roasted, remaindered.
The trains have stopped
they have parked they are
tired. Your voice is so charming;
I look for its accent
under all the couch cushions.

This little friend.
Too much a healthy
fear of the oven. The
kitchen so small, full of
human and mean sentences.
When we are on fire
we are really on fire.

Honey where you been
so long. This shovel
nearly killed my knees.
Consider it done, consider
a change in luggage. Dig a hole
in the farm. This person toward
me. We'll find more potatoes.
Love them on the dollar,
love them to the ground.

Listen Sweetheart. I like you
quiet. I like you in your
flame enduring pajamas.

I like you in December
and you're very pretty in March.
So don't come around here
in summertime, don't dare
come here in June. When I
get myself a pickup truck
play cards with me in the
pickup truck and when we
cannot see to deal no more
we'll go inside we'll go inside
and roast more beets.

ii.

People change. We do
other things in the dark,
these prime doing-it years.
The day the radio tried to
be something else, I raised my
tiny fist to the ceiling and you
are not helping, you are not helping.
The imaginary telephone calls.
We talk about everything and
the darkness how it does us
good, we are up to no good.

The young and the innocent
learn to tolerate themselves.
Cheap beer, pretty teeth.
A good dancer, the shiniest map
there was that night. We get
in and out of our cars like
flashlights. I race to the phone
when it rings. Sick of leaving
all you assholes messages, I
throw my red flags down.
This right here is a place to lie down.

My sister the farm tool, the axe,
the basin. We bring fire for fires.
You don't love me? Do it to a
bedspread of carrots. I'll be
the supermarket. We are still
not special. And when I want you
to know I don't care anymore
I will go like this with my head.
Jesus, I am a bad liar, a bad liar.
In the summer let's go swimming
I will bring my new sunglasses.

Lovely, you really are. What I want
is that you come with me—the
river—watch the river staying put.
One hopes it's sunny and the other
hopes it rains. Either way you'd call it
one-upping. Shenanigans: yes.
Drama, no. Even them most lyrical
animals, let them come and go.

iii.

I don't quite know how to respond here.
It seems our letters are banned in parts of
Georgia. Things find their way back home and the
clouds are more charming than you'll ever be.
I invite the clouds into my bedroom and
they thank me for the hospitality. They thank me
and we sleep. So we started in a bedroom.

When I lived on Killdeer Street I
had the best parties. Important drinks
came down from the fixtures. Like light.
At night when it's quiet I can still
see all the jumping. All the jumping we did.
Marks of hoof love all over the floor,

from all the jumping—what was that if
not a heartbreaking record. Because of an
escape route we are hedging our bets.

Milk was the last thing we needed
this morning. I am sorry, I am sorry.
All this singing and dancing.
Everybody else is doing it and so
so do we. So I said. Let me fall down
in your house and I will never jump again.
What we do to ourselves in the morning
is our secret. Hey Domino, want to go
my way. I'm gonna call you brother.
I'm gonna call you brother tonight.
Making love all the time
just like Bruce Springsteen.

I tried to explain things to the people
but it got dark and chock-full of
foment. Verbs are nothing to me.
You are also nothing to me.
Putting your head in the freezer
is no more safe than putting it in the
oven. Think about it. I am dirty,
I am dirty this morning. Up in the mud
all night. My ears and their new parts.
It's called a Cassette Tape, and you
are not invited, no you are not invited.

On October 8, VOLUBLE
was the word of the day.
A semicircle full of guitars
like a press conference
the day all the wipers stopped
working and I was there and
you were there moreover.
To have a face like that.

As spontaneous as a hill,
I think you're all very special.
The telephone is nothing without
friendship. The grass walks into the
forest. It becomes disoriented.

iv.

Me and my animals we go places
together. Clean Animal Noises in
the Texarkana is a whole
movement of people refusing to
leave their dogs at home. Also,
my father says that beer is
making a comeback. No, he'd say
I'm misquoting. Beer becomes
chichi. What are we gonna do
with all these problems. I will spit
in the face of anyone who says I'm
charming. You don't know charming
from a doorbell. Hello, Hello!
Please let me on in.

Washing the dishes I found good things
to tell you, but I tell you, I've forgotten
it all. This week and next week are the
same anyway. Snow. Melt. We go into
the forest on our lunch breaks and find
what we've been missing. Tight sneakers,
your functioning comb. This right here
is the place where I'd say turn to the
person next to you. Give them
whatever you've got to give.

When the love strike began there was
no cadence. Yes, mountain, I will drive you
to the store. I will write you back. I will

love persistent, I am a good friend.
If I told you the entire story I would
never get it back. Watch me drive this
interstate. I am the best driver when
no one's here. I am faster at being better
as a person, as in a person. This
cadence the way I drive to Fishkill,
Hudson, whatever. What I scratched
into the room this morning:
bite me you big-balled boogie man.
Translate me a haircut there are
translations for everything.

Well I learned what I know about dancing
from Jane Fonda. I said I want you
baby, I said I want some more. Watch me
open this cheap beer with my teeth. Sometimes
there aren't enough goddamn letters in
the alphabet. Looking at the ceiling
we have a Dire Straits situation on our hands
and some radio is just better to listen to
by yourself. We leave because of the weather.
I am ten seconds away from *Automatic for the People.*
Who made who and a nut-suck of feelings.

Puddle on the floor he
looked at me, "Let's
kill a chicken." To
have heard him say
anything was to know
when to go home.
In those days there were
no fiddles. Mama was
a cactus tree. Beneath the trees
snow. Birds in the trees.
Very tiny theater,
you know, sitting all around.
I'll paint your family.
Love and sorrow floating
like a cactus tree.
And we laid down
with people in the
field at the party,
loving each other
all over Cape Cod.
And she runs into the street:
"I like being in America.

Old bicycles, and for what!"
Saying something once
isn't enough sometimes.
Tomorrow is not enough.
Today is a kitchen on fire.
Put me out, put me out.
A person, a person
until proved otherwise.

He said the English word for bagpipe.

I turned into a blanket and went everywhere. With him there was great purpose.

Magic ridden to be a part of. I was the internet one time.

Even the insects in the air had noticed. They were so pensive.

The best part of lying down is the sky I learned and that is what

I learned to wish for.

An understandable problem solver.

A little piece of home.

Sadness comes in bottles and it comes in jars and I let him spread it on me.

I walked when I did I was careful for everything. A special form of season.

In the dark I thought hard I thought Spring and with care I thought of remedies.

The best thing for a person is hand and foot.

What I learned about myself is too much. What I learned for people is too much.

I am a bad person. I go again and again to a room far away.

There are windows and there are great histories. Too much sometimes.

They try again and again and again then some.

Time enough. I am older than I was back then.

Mountains he made me. I was mountains.

But when it came back, water like
banshees, it opened its mouth, received
the lights—we were thrown an excuse in the
form of love letters—the street was called
LOVELY AND EVERYONE. We stayed
decent, our little fork songs all kindled to
green. Tying thunder to winter, he said
beautiful and meant every word: a dog
walk a car ride a moke in the rain. Is this a
great moment? When I was San Francisco
I missed the rock concert, your hair has always
been a hot mess. We could go on a long time like
this, walking notions home from the package store
like dogs. These things I've seen are not
special, the family of jean jackets walks all
over London, they do not know 1988,
they do not know 1988. Honesty a button to
push when scared, people are shit shows of fright.
Time for all the what you want, darlings,
darlings, take the fear from your mouths
and listen, blow on the loveliest lamps.
See the asphalt play moon tiding

games, say it means nothing at all.
This is a message from me, the
messenger, two yellow hearts,
a yellow heart and a blue one.

It feels like the first time. I mean it.
You only get to hold on to something
until you don't hold on to it anymore;
the second part of the holding
is the not holding. To begin with
everything I would like to say: the far
end of the lake, the importance being
the sound of a boat like that, the center of
a lake and those mountains, find flowers,
find sound, find the Italy of the poem.

The lake, the mountains and a vision of
fruit salad. France on a day in June.

It's true. Love made me so angry. Here I am,
a picnic. All spread out on a big lake
lawn. I am a picnic. Sit down and paw
your hands at my basket arrangements.
What mountains? Flowers. Flowers,
flowers. A good story is not necessarily
about two people, it's about fire, or other
moveable things. Astounding electric

hands. *The Decline of the American Empire* for instance. Perspective. Juxtaposition, intrigue. Maybe she used to be a little more beautiful. A couch in a country house is a second long in length. Swift movements. A repetition of a kiss-kiss to say, It's Nothing. The weather, the weather! A lake and its mountains. A small boat because it's hard to get anywhere. Like France. Something rough and hard that will break your face open. If it's raining, we'll just have to learn how not to get wet.

Sounding boat of the lake
a little bridge and a woman
standing. Talloires. Things
like a perimeter. A lake and
mountains to form a perimeter.
Also, three weeks in summer,
colors showing 1970. Water
to the sky I look at you. Sounding
motor, red and blue and green.

*

How a boat comes in
and away and how to look
at a young girl. These old
country houses. Like a
couch, wallpaper. Something
must be done. The tree
like mountains.

*

In the nettles we find
our nothings. Nothing
happening as a happening
in the nettles. The mother
in Nancy. Brown red blue.
The water as wallpaper.
The weather always
as something to say.
The weather says,
you're lovely, the
weather says don't go.

*

How a woman runs
into the summer, running.
Do you smell the lake?
The color of upset the
lake smells cold. A
hand in a hand as
a holding, so little,
like the honesty
of young people. I've never
tired of you. Come back
for me when I've
become mean.

*

For instance, today
is wonderful again
and flowers. Again
the wallpaper as
water. Red yellow
pink white. A man
in a tie, a man in
a suit, a handsome
man in a suit and tie.

*

The water as a way
of carrying people.
Smile, sweetness. To
not agree. Mountains
and a grand perspective.
This weather and
the mountains.

*

How a certain
dress and a certain
shoe can make a girl.

However old she's
become complicated.

*

Monday, July 6
green yellow blue
and them bounding
down the mountain.
Seen from below. Love
and a picnic, the
man wore brown.
Dead in the center
the lake is sound.
There, a comfort
found in impossible
forms of love.

*

These reckless behaviors,
your trusting shoes.
Was that a subway,
were we in France?
Chin on the crown
of the head, what
other maneuvers. Let's
list the ways to do it
in white glory. "She's
very nice." That hair,
wild and full, young lady
young lady. When he tries
to kiss you do not pull
away. Even Paris sometimes,
let me cover your face, I
want to tell you something.

*

White blue red green
and a bench. "So I
behave" sending the
little love letters away.
I can't say much but
I love him—I can't say
why but it's instinctive,
I promise. Come at me
with flowers and I will
run away. I manage a
factory of self-preservation.
It's like I've found you
again in the factory.
Be small and feel good,
sounding boat red and
blue, like an anthem of
curiosity the pointlessness
of green. To learn from
our littles. Buttoned
as if the weather
were not July.

*

Not quite the meeting
in white and clay. How
do you contact an
island anyway? You're
better than tennis, I
know how to stay here.
To stay as an act just as
much as to go. He will
have to go on. We can't
have the story ending
here in its middle.

*

To own a thing from
your very desire. Yes,
different kinds of wanting.
It would have been
easier to pin her down
the apartment floor.
I'm sure you've noticed
all these thin delicate girls.
What will happen to them
by the time they're thirty.
Wallpaper, green
plants and flowers.

*

Desire to follow
possession to herd
without hands,
Sorceress, what can
you do? "I'm the camp
director, and campers
have complained!"
Ugly on the mountains
gestures can do anything
blue green yellow
"there were people
swimming there" the
mountains saw and angry.
White white white
white green.

*

There were people
swimming. And if
something more
didn't happen you
are the fault of that.
I'm really getting married,

trees and the mountains like
wallpaper. Mountains and
a red chair, then Tuesday.
Tender of course, it
doesn't matter.

*

The clouds as
wallpaper and the
weather as narrative
I do not value
your opinion. The
patience of looking
at one thing and no
other. I saw the
afternoon and it lied
to me, the sky and the
water as one muted
shade. These feelings,
awkward as business,
green red wallpaper
as wallpaper. The
precision of a thing
like a gesture. I hate
to make anyone cry.

*

Friendship on a
couch as wallpaper,
you, magician, as
my friend. There are
few occasions to look
at the camera. We are
seen, we are counted
as necessary things.

*

Good-bye lake and
good-bye mountains,
little red boat and
hot-tempered story.

When I was in the devil's room I cried.
I found rotating bridges because timing works differently in
    Prophetstown, Illinois.
I cried. Care. Care. Care. Care.
The paintings, the stars. That is what wounded looks like.
The waves are clouds and oceans. Dear Michigan, hands like a fish.

A pool like any other, it is 1987. Who knew we would be stories.
Little girl, little girl not so close to the edge.
Country politics that could fit in New Jersey. We were fun.
We were fun/not fun then. Fishes of the sea and
mountains like a family, 1987 as two very nice
connecting rooms. "Hey little girl what station do you
listen to?" *Rock.* I find this very confusing.
Let's see if they can stand to talk to one
another. The weather as always in charge.

Clouds fiery, like a
problematic bear, we
color these afterthoughts
random, like appetite. As
happens with any absence,
some things will no longer be
that monster, a person greets
nightmare when they become
nightmare. So

he was no longer my
monster, I was no more a
season, the little lights round
and thunder. Field and fence
like a brothering, the hair
coming home you dropped a
stone in a field. Frankly it can't
matter. Animal or image as
interruption, a thing itself,
a possibly returning feature,
you always wanted an
island. In the rain we got
angry. I named you Field,
you brought me flowers,
we broke our necks on
small time.

A little field of bodies, as if
color had what to do with
victory, that smallest decision
to answer the phone at night, for
example, lift plain receiver to mouth
and engage in fear, sure quiet

noise: I saw a good movie, yes,
and steak dinner, how is your
mother, I went with an almost
stranger, yes, it was just what
I wanted. The quietest

step in a direction, that
is what I mean. A small
piece of island made sound for
the ages when the lightning
meets its train, monster song is the
best remedy—like bird magic,
I fell into a suitcase and was dancing.

This mighty arrow and I are going straight
to the moon tonight. Don't try to stop me.
I guess I just want things that are certain.
So when I say I have had an overmuch
don't let go of me. I say dumb shit all
the time. I don't know if I would make a
good fisherman but I know what place is
and I know the many kinds. The kind like
a kitchen table, the kind like a beach
in a pretty country. The kind like the
blanketed self hovering above
some road someplace because Honesty is
making up stories and sticking to them.
Like driving a car, or wearing a swim-
suit, make it special, Sweetheart. The hair like
a piece of home, you can do whatever
you want to me. Like driving a car, or
wearing a swimsuit. See how I manage
all the fire when it comes in little circles.
Pink particles kill one pink particle
at a time. There are these moments we are
missing entirely. I sat behind

a really pretty boy in France, I wanted
to kiss his neck. Nighttime is for sleeping,
that's when you're supposed to sleep. And the
Devil's Vegetables should be prepared like
you're cooking in Denver. Remember
that the size of this aircraft is indicative
of just how big dreams can be. I shine. I
keep trying. I mean, why not, I am out
of small slips of paper and if Stevie
Nicks can be broken-hearted then so can
I. I'm going to get red tights. No. No
no, I will sit right here. If I ever wear
lipstick I'd like it to be "June Bride."

REGARDLESS OF RIVERS, AGGRESSION IN THE DRIVEWAY
IS UNLOVELY

By razor blades
I'm bleeding.
I love London in July!
The Riviera!
But I am serious.
A standoff.
And if something fell
into my arms
I would take it.
I know boats
and you're no boat,
and this, what to say:
little wild orchard.

*

Green yellow lamps,
a yellow house. Seven
windows, eight to
count the attic. The
trees, the way things
could have been. Ivy
like a rash, here I am,
home and beautiful,
the sky almost in
the evening. Maybe
there were crickets.
Girl in a big chair.

*

The car turns over at
night. A dress for picking
flowers. For sitting

here. Catch this
blanket, lay it down
and see. To stand
and declare with your
hand on your hip.
Like we're listening,
like we're even listening.

*

To go out into the boat,
the spine of the river, it was
dusk and spoiled for love.
To mean something, like
a green fireplace, impatient
shoes. Pink jacket in a window
and rude. I am trying to
find something tiny and mute.
Underwater and in France.

*

Advance and retreat
advance and retreat,
these people and the things
we've put flowers in.

*

So really this is
a film about beauty.
And meanness. And
once again, France. Let me
tell you a story—

*

A little white lamp and the same
country couch, I listened to you.
Several buttons on every sleeve,
a quiet room. Terrible furniture

and love will make it better.
I will pour two glasses. I will
give you the bigger one.

*

Some things
will always look
like this. We had
a lovely time and
a deep chair. Ugly
speaks to Lovely
and somewhere
else people make
terrible histories.
Intolerable love.

*

Impossible hand,
we go to sleep.
Everyone thinks it's
funny. Everyone wearing
the little blue bathroom.
Two people and
a broken thing
as a road somewhere.
We both wore velour!
I went home to that big
country house, I took off
my clothes and I did not
sleep. I waited for
something and its
window. A room and
window. Are we done?
Did you find your shoes?
A blue shirt and white
pants, you are handsome
under a tree and next to the

shade. This is where I said,
Let's Kill A Chicken,
where I threw down all
of those rocks. These are chairs
and those are tables. Tables and
chairs. The telephone is black
and means something, in fact,
it means a lot; the plainest
people just listening.

I wanted something and I
couldn't tell you today. I will
consider myself a window.

All these tools we have for
saving people—just don't
let go of me. Sometimes in

this world you see things you
don't want to see. Sometimes
the entire ground is shaking

and there's no trace of any
more flowers standing. A
thing of the past has come

to knock everything over.
Flowers could be perfect
rivers despite their various

weathers, requests. Daisies might
bark, and let them. Roses are
boring as anything yellow

is bored by being put next to
the sun. Lilies sound prettier
than that. So let's just call this

delicacy. And the oceans grow
stars inside, and flowers. This is
not difference. A vegetable

stand is more different than
all of this. More than anything,
punishment is punishment and

I really just wanted to talk to you.
Like a repetition of a time,
California. We went walking—is

this boring? We went walking for
sandwiches—is this? And it
was California and my sweater,

electric, seen so far away, I was also
electric and we were electric we were
wet electric because it was raining.

Said, find us, alignment
could well mean
please, find us. Control is not
for me. To learn from
all kinds of music! What harm
could be had. The multitudes of
secret handshakes, high hopes
kill every time. Dangerous
accumulations and mistakes
in the weather. I never
saw such a broken-in window
but last night it was a yellow
car. The mechanic gets
laid why he smells like that.
We have no control. The screens
bad enough for Japanese
ladybugs. This Land. Where
else is the weather such a
conversation where else does the
weather sound so much
like this. Prophets of a square
of a land this big. They say
big sky go south and west, they
say water, pick your best hand,
drive that way they say moose
and you would be so lucky
they say corn maze, you say how
high they say jello you
say pretty how beautiful
I could eat this every day. The
apartment, the apartment. The
floor is failing by the slippers'
count. O kind fixtures, O sweet

light. To have guests to
put it out. Weather make
me talk less weather say the
lovelies. In the dining room, cloudy
with a dew point of blue flowers.
Said Come Over to the armchair, won't
you. What else could I have
said to the shower. The airplanes
audible. What kind of forecast.
What a picture this is becoming.
Shapes are difficult to speak of.
Shiny protective material. All these little
mishaps. Quiet! Quiet riot in the city.

I say what I see.
It's just that simple.
It is night out and
beautiful. O face,
seriously, I
miss you like horses.
What I learned is
consequences. The
same people, the same
people every place
cock their heads for
everything possible
to come over. Sometimes
people say "I like your
boots" because they don't
know what else to say.
Peg and Satan were
shipping things, trying
to do right by people.
Boxes are things to
hug without responsibility.
Like a road in Concord

turns because you know
it will, I know what
all this means because
I'm telling you about it.
Dear Americans,
You run better
than French people fish.
Seriously, like horses.

All torn up and the babies

turned cold and we planted

things to keep things

warm. It was that morning

I took my coffeepot

back from the closet.

But what will we do with

all these potatoes?

And so the narrative:

I loved. I loved a lot of them

a lot. I arranged visits and

we failed. Don't be sad.

My liver is clean and I kicked

that sugar habit. I may go

swimming this afternoon. The lake

on my hair. You have apple hair

and I threw a pancake in the river.

Come on, I'm exciting to be with you.

I said, I've got a live dandelion.

And I drive us home and

I reach for your hand

and you give it to me

and it is sweet, held.

And on my street we go

for a walk and you are

charming it is summer

and you are charming.

Of all the other times

I've said this sort of thing

this time I mean it

I mean it the most. You are

the most fun. I love your

hands in the air. We are good

to each other and you

tell me lots of things. What it

means to love people in all

this glory light. How you came

to dance in little circles and that

the way into a monster is

short and terrible. We go

swimming. October, be

gentle, be good pizza. A

nice visit. We will want

to do this more than once.

There is a park down the street.

And we put our hands up

to lie down, there is a field to lie us

down, lying down in the dark.

A stern man and
a building. A car.
To drive, à conduire,
in the mountains. To
take prayer seriously with
your serious face. A
serious woman you
imagine loving. She has
a headband on.

*

To follow, à suivre,
getting stuck all
the time in France.
Determination, say that.
Math in France is math.
Even in the Chanturgue Hills.

*

Again she would be
his wife. On a bicycle
and in France. Passion as
a bother. Upstairs! Upstairs!

*

Math as a way to
prove social existence,
I'm not interested
(blah blah blah blah).
After mass let's go see
this divorced lady.
The singing masses.

*

Uncomfortable dinner. The
little girl gets up from bed.
To be delighted, little lights.

*

Isn't everything nice!
To know how to
clear a table, spot the
dream bicycles, spot
the clouds on a ramp.

*

I am a stern man and
uncomfortable with myself.
(Blah blah math out the
windows always snow.)
And awkward they sit there,
the two of them (blah
blah cigarettes) the
vaulted ice cream (blah
blah lie down) to recline,
de se reposer, on a
bed with a divorced
woman. There is talking
and he demotes himself
to the chair.

*

Ha ha ha in a bedroom.
People lean in closer. To tell the
saddest stories. Yes, it's absurd
in front of a naked woman.
She has beautiful eyes and
hair—what's wrong with
you, stern man. To put on

a tie, tiny or not, I could be your
big brother, that animal blanket.

*

To the countryside.

*

You are worthwhile,
he says to the girl.
Saulzet. They talk about
danger, driving in weather and
math. He is proud of himself.

*

The most romantic offer in the
snow. We don't always qualify.
(I'm not Catholic, not blonde.)
We would make a perfect couple
in the snow.

*

Toulouse. I am leaving
Clermont. The stern man
most handsome in the kitchen.
Blinking little lights. To talk
of marriage, to be hypothetical.
If you like to think the wind then think it.

*

To see how a man is on a road,
icy in the country. My car has also
been stuck in the snow. (To
show breasts more often, make
tea, Clermont.) "I don't make friends
easily." Careful careful, we are so careful.

*

The stern man in another
kitchen. Things discussed
in a kitchen. Turtleneck on the
face. Disappointment, then Church.

*

The wallpaper a city,
dear man, you win.

*

To love each other in snow,
Clermont, Toulouse, to love
each other in the dunes.

Here again, yellow
cloud as big white sneakers.
And always the window.
And that person's window
and that person's window.
June lays down a garden
of beer and Patience
catches fireflies in a
jar. I don't care what time
it is, all I know is
Patience is catching
fireflies in a jar. People don't
like questions when they
don't know the answers,
the fireflies dressed up
like pretty fighting stars.
The window says TREE
back at all of us looking
and whatever it doesn't say
makes us want to say more.
Plain, let me tell you about
the flowers I'm growing:

I came up when the moon was
still showing and there were
sirens in the middle of the street,
like country yellow houses.
Listen to her barely open her mouth.
There's no irony in this.
He leaned in and I leaned in
and everyone kissed. His teeth
smelled like the beach. These
frank sounds of hours like
somebody's skin. I got here
a long time ago and want you
to stay. We all want you to stay.
And suddenly, CHILDREN!
I cannot win. Once I get
these boots on, I will not
take them off. I'm scared
I'm also excited.

Last night I had a bad dream and
you were like always. In and out

of the house there were backpacks
packed. I'll stay here. It's mine.

A bird's nest our home. You could
be a narrative. We can

keep talking. There are delicacies in
history. Ways of speaking.

Terms of phrase. The sounds of pants.
Do you trust me. Because I

stutter and I care a whole lot.
When we watch movies we are

looking for trouble. We are looking
to be told we know better than that.

Let the child out of the backseat
at the train station. Around us are
white fields and we say nothing,
we sell staircases and buildings.
Balloons. Let's say repetition is very
bright. Muddy river. Dead dog. The
terrible terrible. My stolen car in
the hearts of others.

Emboldened to wear white I will
sleep tonight with all the lights on. This
all ends badly like weather we can't
understand. Sometimes when no one's
looking, I dance inside my bones—a
little something left to feed the
story, I am a terrible river but with you
I was a yellow shoe holding open a door.
Riding around in the park like a ship
the car was only itself.

My little sisters, don't you know
about elephants, how they're like

windows, especially broken with helmets
on as if thunderstruck, just waiting
for you to pull up in a wagon.

What I found in the river
is the night we found each other.
Quiet, green, he lay down, my
head hurt like the top of a train,
a dog shaking clouds out of the sky.
I wear a helmet so you don't hurt
me, I wear a helmet to keep a
heart. I am a small raincoat, you
are the weatherman. Fall down,
fall down. I mean the woods.

Mistaking the thing itself,
a season moves its only
mouth to the next and
if winter never happens,
don't watch me thinking
of the last thing that
wrecked, the difficult
improbably, bad snacks we
left upstate, unbecoming.
However more I could tell anyone
what didn't happen to me, I'd tell
them precisely what did. Dear
get dressed, go out from the
house, engage the grave
streets in their permanent
attire. The mind still waters
just what it can and you are
always on the bashed side of
the issue; no one needed
to stand in for rope because
rope was doing just fine.
Beaver root, cow lily, bonnets,

lesser duckweed, what I need
is to know why I keep these
mugs. Like you're ready, hold
on to yourself, run into the fields
with your new fast shoes, your
best friends waiting to let you
on in. If I make a fool turn the
lamplight over, I'm not going home
without a piece of that sky.

That there could ever be
a blue that shines so well
into a yellow! The blue and
the yellow all suddenly a new
kind of color. What are
the children doing? Are they
working on that maple tree?
So much here can't be
said just yet. A person has to
feel something to believe it.
If a person has a face
it could be very hard for
that person to imagine
having another face.
Does anyone understand
anything? Two benches
are two people. Words are
kinds of special to any
body. The wall is full
of flowers, all kinds of
prairie flowers. Hope
is a smell more than

anything. (It smells like
hope and it is a quick
smell.) The most beautiful
honesty can't decide
which way she wants
to go from her home in
the country. "I need eggs
and the library" she says.
What is a person to do
with all the time. Talk dirt
into the ground. Shouting
is banned in some
countries. A whisper,
a gesture in kindness.
People are just people
and they love them
nonetheless.

I am your friend. I go deeper into the forest.

I put a belt on, I make out with bandits to see if you care.

This is what it's like in heaven. The animals cutting our hair.

When they dance it looks like they just want to feel something.

The happy happy bird!

We are human kites and we eat breakfast.

Can you fire the wind?

No. You cannot. You are just a person in California.

In the forest birds stop. They become broccoli.

I can convince myself of anything.

And the wind ruined your face.

Everyone was disappointed and I was toothpaste.

Dear me. This is what fireworks look like.

A thing to complicate stars.

You love like a slow train coming to a stop.

A bird walks into a bar and lies down in the grass.

If I touch the bird and it is afraid.

If I touch the bird and it is afraid of everything.

And to begin with
the familiar, brown
fence. Silence but birds
to show we are listening.
Pageboy, but a girl opening
the gate, a woman, the
most woman, driving.

*

In immediate stakes,
(beach, no beach) there are
hydrangeas. A white table
and a difference in ages.
No, no love, I have never
been in love. Let us say
there is magic in that.
Everyone dressed
in white like a job.

*

An admittance of age
in the form of marriage.

*

The beach is cold, an old
friend windsurfing, sexy
as a wetsuit, he loves her.
But how another man might
win her eyes, a red shirt,
white pants. Dressed,
and the less dressed.

*

Everyone fell in the style
of Brittany. Like a bow, red
for a danger.

*

A woman like a chair. This
vague woman talks love
like a tease, like a bow is
affixed to her mouth.
A fireplace talks of burning,
talk in the form of flirting,
a doll smiling, stupid doll.
And then the women look
at us, the girl gets up from the
hearth, assumes central position
to stare at us looking.

*

Variations on bald men to show
where we are in life.

*

When I'm six and you're
twelve, of course not,
never. But when I'm
thirty, won't you find me.
I warned you, I might not be
any fun tonight, even if
we go dancing.

*

I push myself against the
wall to kill the stupid from
your mouth. If you were a
friend you'd never say such
nonsense. You kiss stupidly,
the not-known defeating

the known already.

*

There are surfing lessons.

*

The girl finds a boy
perhaps her own age.
The doll goes for sex, sex
with Dressed. Red is elected
central character. She
teases, she looks harsh
in red. I think he will take
off her swimsuit, don't you.

*

Doll in the hedges not
knowing. Less-dressed
all in white knowing
everything. The telling
bushes, a tactless
suggestion. Talking to someone
about someone else to show
all the ways that you love them.

*

As if people slow danced
to classical music, she
runs upstairs and expects
to be followed. Manipulating
color, all these people
in white are lying.

*

A mountain town
behind a car, what
could be better than

beautiful, remember
breathing.

*

People look for sounds
of a woman. Infidelity
toweled in a window,
some people look like
snakes, they do.

*

I would love you as a rule
if only you weren't as you are.
The beach again, the sea.

*

A red bow again, and
women fighting.

Honesty toward the face,
a softer version of lies,
dull pretending.

*

Hydrangea breakfast
these women and
flowers, a doll before
bushes as the most stupid.
A telegram lights
the narrative, see how
she spits into the note.

*

The red and white man wakes
confused, dons a robe.
He's off to meet someone
in Spanish. The uniforms

battering, the man is
inappropriate, what he
does to her legs.

Recollection consuming, the
conundrum calling on special,
willing the dark, the deer, their
blown paths to the showering of
instant demise. One of the nights
the sky fell over, came home, put his
keys in the jar. I am the Ostrich in the
foyer, I think about death a lot in general.
What I want from you is necessary
but I don't know how to ask. Do I
put my coat on first, or at the same
time? I hate assuming, Molasses,
you love too slow. While you're still
in this world you are what you want
to be, the woman, the weather, a
woman like a picture I am 1929
and I look all right as a mother:
organized. You're older than that.
At least in this bright lifetime
we'll get to know the forest, the
moon and what about the moon,
a window toward other things, trees

for example. On the other hand, look at
broken fire making out in the shed.
I'm sorry this package does not contain
tiny horses, next time, friend.

I can be happy for you and your bad taste. I can do right by you. It's
    fun out here in the dark.

The disequilibrium in the conception of any one room. The
    chandelier and window treatments!

An intriguing form of closeness. Of love. If I prick your arm

do you even have feelings.

Quick, dress me in the loveliest things.

Feelings in the forest in the car in your bed are to be kept. Keep the
    singing close.

Learn what you can and quietly. Keep the change, kid, spend it later.

I will tough you up I will leave you for dead I will put words in
    your dead mouth.

To sleep outside as practice for the day the house burns down.

Who left the candles so close to the paper towels, who'd do that.

Walk on me a minute. Let me lose my breath a little.

I will spend summers with you.

An animal sits at its desk and tries to do right by you.

It just doesn't seem natural. The animal lies down in protest.

All we have is pronouns. And light. And light.

Something like an ocean lives in the grass.

We come here to understand
especially little things.

Two birds are dancing.
Can you hear their
wings brushing on the
hallway floor? It is like
tiny imaginary sweetness.
Like the part of a shadow
intended only for sound.
Look look look look
look look look,
you can see it.

Sometimes the house is
just not enough and thoughts
are undressed into feelings.

France is grand today. 1986
was just like this: giving our
grapefruits little suntans.
These days young people
don't give a damn. Yarrow?
What does that even mean.
Family commitments?
Like a tub? I'm a metropolitan
woman! A woman who buys
a lamp because it suits her.
Maybe I'm ordinary,
huffed against a fence post.
I'd like to be both of us
at the same time. You
looking here at you.

It begins on a train
because she is thinking
and people take trains
to get places. Hair wild and
full, this young lady is older,
an older building takes her in.

*

We wear sweaters because
they are beautiful, we lie
on beds to make phone calls.
Lamp lit for night scene, the
phone rings and ruins everything.

*

She goes into the shower
and disappointment.
Someone has a son, a
son galloping horses.
Yes, wives and kids as
disappointment. Yes
too many paintings at
the painter's studio. This
is not my house, she says, I am
going home, I am getting married.

Leaving the painter, she wishes him
well and many mistresses.

*

In Le Mans she finds her
car, drives a road invisibly.

*

In a store for antiques,
say Friday. Pretty mouth, say
that. Her friend making
lamps, helping us through.
To no one in particular, it's
more of an idea, marriage,
the stubborn girl knows
what she wants, she knows
there are men everywhere.

*

A beautiful street, she's
very impulsive. A white
house with flowers to remind us
of color. The bohemian in me
is over, she says. Dear Society,
which milieu do you mean.

*

Honest friend I like you
in the daytime, I don't like
you with your family. At the
wedding, she says, I won't stay
long, always they depress me,
I have so much to read! A horn
sounds, listen to the street.

*

The road takes in,
it is practical. You could
wear your black dress,
I will wear my red one.

*

She goes to the wedding,
an extraordinary dress.
His name is two glasses please.
She compels herself to honesty
and they talk like they've just
met. Jersey porcelain is so
hard to find. Consider these
moments the wind rivals
color. He's needed on the
telephone—would you apologize
for me—her face in the window
watching color and the wind,
all forms of disappointment.

*

Lightning arranges, just call
him, this lawyer. I have some
porcelain for you, she says,
I'll pick you up on Sunday.

*

Not in the same manner,
it is Sunday, she is driving.
Not Louis' son, but Paul's;
this vase is for my mother.

*

Frankly in the car she says
what she wants to. They go
to a restaurant, his eyes like
disappointment; the jokes
pass each other like dogs at
night. She leans him into a
bridge, a take in.

*

The antiques Madame is angry: Jersey,
Jersey! I'm really getting married.
She looks to the left and quits
her job, good business sense or not.

*

In church she prays and runs
into a man. Setting little candle
fires, stained glass is careful too.

*

Notice. I want to be a
housewife. Before a window
she can do anything, young lady,
anything. Marriage as the pooling
of a couple's talents, wallpaper as
this truth. She insults the world,
happy she wants.

*

Mother this impending marriage,
mother, these ideas. She is
done giving in, giving over.

*

Invisible street forming
ideas, impatience as a way
to take the train. The
street invisible for more
ideas, a birthday party
a place for song.

*

He is late, she's in tears,
and he has a case in Narbonne.
Smiling, show where to
put a gift, show how
much you care.

*

Impetuous family. Hair
such a mess in Paris, she
goes back to the country,
she will not call. She wants
a man to hold on to, she
needs only a minute.

*

No time, he says, even for
apology. No, she didn't get
the letter, the telephone
interrupting, I'm awfully
busy, he says to her, wait
a minute, I will tell you.

*

"I left when I was
uncomfortable."

"But all eyes were
on me, it was my
birthday."

"But I'm terribly
independent, I will
not tie myself
to another."

*

She apologizes for the
bother. He issues a small
warning, says he's not in
love with her—she says

a dally, not you, me

and god, his brave
comparison—her to
a country house he
likes a lot. Should I buy it, he
asks her standing there, even
if I don't feel like being
in the country?

*

"Don't go away now, angry."

"I'm not angry. What
made you think you were
what I wanted!"

*

Before this tapestry
she feigns disinterest.
Shouts hypocrite chicken.

*

On the train she is
happy at the window,
the colors of the country.
A wild woman, she goes
back to Le Mans, returns
to the lovely invisible street and,
like other women, makes lamps.

Under the stars, shining faces. The faces holding on.

1986 was just like this.

The look was completely ethereal,

the new towns, ethereal.

We came here to understand

a person from another time.

We would later call him

the American Triangle.

A tender soul, he has no telephone.

He laid it all out, like

fabric could be a woman,

like Kate Bush looking for a teapot, big eyes.

A screaming man lying down in a field.

In Cleveland I think he

would have been beautiful

and in 1997 he gave me clouds.

Time like pink minutes, the man

sits down his head in a glass. Says

nice things. Say a river.

Like a beacon, a raincoat,

he danced like the fastest

windshield wipers, sitting

happy for the window's sense
of self. To feel the telephones
ringing. I am so tired. Can I
say that? Can I say that I saw
a rainbow and it wasn't raining,
that there was nothing wet
in the sky? The ocean is a place
and so is the heart, the heart
a place worth living. Don't
look at me, I'm failing.
Cry, goddamn it, cry.

If all I have to give you
is this, then you aren't
what I wanted. My wall a
rubber band, I'm shattered.
The papier-mâché meteor spills
that which used to think
of us; nothing is scarier
than animals in moonlight,
mirror in the bathroom,
what do you want from me.
We're not sleeping, not
dancing and rations from
the basic barricade confirm
immaculate cities need it
just the same. You unfortunate,
remembered animal holding
pines, sing at will, take me to
the public library, a lot.
Put me in your hand and
row, right here, touch here:
touch clear and touch clock,
enjoy your microwave.
Rise up, wind, show us

what you see. It could
be the ocean but perhaps
it's a song. Sing, then, song,
up into the vestibule,
climb into the small lit
ceiling not yet keeping us in.

OUR FLOWERS ARE CALLED WATERFLOWERS
AND THEY NEED A LOT OF WATER

It's so hard to know that we are done with a lot of what we have been.

For any of us, made from something, made anything.

Made a little wooden boat and a little wooden horse and

a little, little ocean worth swimming.

The rivers are calling and the telephone brings mackerel, cooked well,

home. A bird takes off its clothes and goes down to the water.

Of all the perfect gestures, be good at naked.

In the morning, be pinecones.

Listen, grass stains, successful futures don't start here.

Send more flowers. Friendly gestures all the way to the ocean.

Bring the fields their winnings, bring the rooms their people.

Don't walk away! I thought the grass was moving. I mean, I saw it moving.

What would he say to all of this mess, this mess of a river.

I am so much more than pants! Legs on fire from all the night tonight.

I see trouble. It has a sweet voice. You can

tell trouble by the sound of its voice. The world is full

already, let's keep our voices down.

And you had your lower

retainer in, you said

beautiful. There was

kissing, a basement, you

were handsome, I was

frightened, lacking

shoes among the rusty nails,

you said don't worry.

We disrupted violin lessons

then a crowd of

hideous men came in,

we had not locked the

door. You should always

lock the door to a party, some

big men carry guns. You held

like holding was the only part

of you working and I'm glad

that you came to the party, thank you

for still coming to parties at night.

Under the small staircase

we went again, the towering

trombones. Some can't help

petrified thoughts, at

least we help them try—

a forest in the bravest

places, the gratitude of fear—

I run, I run, you don't run.

I was also broken so I took him in. It's a small island.
A horse woman painting a white horse to show all the colors.
Let me tell you, her skin is beautiful. There are other
kinds of money and we could be better for the masses.
Empty the house and keep going. If I hold the pillow and
you listen, you are the ocean. Oh, Sweet Flag, lying
in the field like anything living lying down, come here!
You can pick berries on your way. Nothing clarifies
like more kisses, and the stone hurt the river by being
in the way. I am the river in my own way.
Pull up the woods and see. Imagine the weather,
preindustrial and mostly religious, somebody's uncle
alone in a jar catching light. Romance on account of
intruder as animal. Intruding animal. I am not going
to consciously promote myself. I will not show
cleavage very often. Women should really
talk to one another. When I was an
almond, some people don't need people.

Intersection of France
and a blue car, the slow state
carries no one. New houses
they are white, they are blue,
running feet, the proverb
announces: something regarding
houses and women. The colors
prove November.

*

Bow, big hair, big coat,
blue and red to prove
each other, gray and red
all the same. Lies in the
country, lies. Compromise
as the height of devotion
I won't make anyone do that.

*

The little voice walks out
the door, red scarf good-byes,
they take the train, these
dark-haired women, office
beautiful. Coats in the closet
and scarves, she has a
secret apartment she hides
from her home in the suburbs.
Fancy Paris.

*

To not seem handy
on account of the ether,
blue red gray black, he's

up to something. And
all the new towns that
happened in the eighties, they
make me feel like dying, like
flying to France and dying.

*

We all need time alone, Louise.

*

Private, public reverie,
I wouldn't live with anyone.
Having skipped loneliness
entirely, she solves her own she
paints the apartment, Paris
will do for a secret. When
cotton was the best shape, me too,
me too.

*

Red couch, the city
makes us put coats on,
take them off again. Coat
performance, wrapping paper,
surprise, the birthday, the
dress, strap-zippers.

*

Terribly planted, people
configuring life before another,
he tries to seduce her she
almost laughs it's like she's
laughing. All of us, beasts
some of the time.

*

One woman green, one in
white, party chitchat, what
they wear to demonstrate
a body. Another making lamps,
they have strong faces, I never
want to leave this party. And
when her boyfriend walks to
her, she looks like death, the
face of death, big drapes
in a tall room in France.

*

From one to another
"Don't stop her from
dancing!" Talk they knew
they'd have—if you're
bored then go already—
the tiny lady crying,
a real treat, I'm not angry,
they always say that, but
then they're always lying.

*

Everything ruined the car,
a way home, women
discussing violence and
whether men want to love.
An ethics in the carried,
glass blue door, the handles,
he looks like a French vampire.

*

She knows it will make him
mad, she says it anyway.
I am painting my apartment
and I want to live there, I like
my furniture. To be like that,

sitting on a chair saying things,
blue red flowers that prove
two o'clock, I never married the
others but let me live alone
I could love you forever. A calm
absurd discussion like when a
boy and I used to compromise,
but that was a long time ago
and in the U.S.A.

*

December, a trunk, a painting.
How many rooms in a month,
gray and red, the bedded telephone,
repetition as our only friend.
Plans broken, make new plans.
A green book, acquaintances,
what to do with ourselves,
it was museums we wanted.

*

Breakfast with cassette tapes.

Begotten teapots.

Wow, he says in France.

*

January, a smaller room, her
friend immediately talking.
His eyes too big he speaks
of the terrified fields, just
beautiful, she washes her
hands, momentary Poland,
she does not want to exit the
bathroom, the restaurant of
my sister's 16th birthday.

I take off my socks at
this point in the movie.

*

The business of lamp making,
incredible bulbs the colors of
a game of colors. To hear and
not hear at the same time,
ahora mismo, I am not Spain.

A discussion of indefinite
articles, the train station
expressing new colors.

*

February dancing in a
small black dress.
The kitchen kissing
orange juice, some
friendships dwell on
planet danger. The
last train home
sounded hands. I can't
tonight, call tomorrow.

*

Little apple, why are you
so green, tomorrow a message,
impatient machine.

The detectives we are, a way
to make shame garden
on the face, her friend
ridiculous: if I'd slept with you,
nonsense. People confusing
each other to no end.

*

Moon, a bike ride, coffee
then dancing and while
the moon is still they
sleep. She cannot sleep
—she takes her bag and
coat bravely—she leaves
the apartment. Plaid men
introduce the full moon.

*

Let's just say it didn't work,
the apartment arrangements.
She goes home to the country, on
the first train, her boyfriend not
there, where, blue door, did you
sleep last night. When she looks
out the windows it's like looking
forever, not more just different.

And here is where it says

one summer was hard.

Something concerning bruised

lilac, drowned hickory. Then

something about a concert, it

was small, there were trumpets

and animals in the field, man's

face like a carriage, certain. Supposing

dress, it describes better ways to get

naked, wet shoes and stockings

worth solving. Brave, green

explains the morning, the part

about the violent age and weather

becoming a friend who stops

by to inquire. A tooth falls

out in hell. Blood evidence,

the shirt bleeds, it says the

marks were halting and how

the family prayed. The ocean

brought itself back to the country,

managed to stay, maneuvering

triumph in the face of decay.

Water carries flowers into the fields,

it says something then about that.

I had an angry period: for
the trees to fall down on the
floor, the room of vantaged
things, however long you can
keep this hold you can stay.
I was, one could say, the time of
the clouds, rivers, ocean and
mountains—I forgot the
fields—all of these things to hold
starry mouths. So you cannot
stop, no, you mustn't, bordered
and partial, I will put things in my
mouth: lucky chair, undone legs
and everyone sitting together
a while, dear attempt to be
cooperative, say frequency,
camera, ligature, blue. Blush
the room and it will live, leave it
cold and nothing; stay by the
weather to see if the weather and
if only there's always tomorrow.
The treatise of your friend and
all of his friends, all of our friends
nothing. Thundersnow doesn't
mean anything if you aren't
looking outside and like ice
we aren't sorry. You touched
my leg and assumed things, so
we assumed things for days, stopping
for gas and market snacks, you
were a dream, with your long hair

and your eyes. I keep these thoughts
of you having fun, they turn into stoves
and my friend the painter says, if you
paint it red people are going to like it.

Shame gets out of bed for
no one in particular and there's
nothing wrong with that. We say things
until we don't want to anymore.
That is called broken, it's
called desire. If the room
were another half itself more, if
the trees were quieter when they
grouped together talking and if a city
was in my house and you were in that
city. Well anything just about ends
when we fall down at night. Having
moved toward victory, I was ready to
lie on the floor until it was all over.
Waiting the forest out, we spoke
I think you kissed my arm. Darkness
finds a meticulous hole and falls asleep
inside; my mouth has little corners.
See, return is just another word for
shame—no, virtue, molecule? Blight.
The ghosted things we used to do as
beggars for the waves still make good

stories but stories come with graph paper,
graph paper with song. I could show you
something but I don't want to, I have to
keep my coat on, I have to
take us home. The pin light at
the end of my mind flashes off
like it just had to. Color as your new
best friend, I asked you what you're
still doing here, you said you wanted fire.

IMAGINARY POEM

Just as much as there
ever was, this will be
for the time there was
a river in your hair on fire.
Perimeter of stolen fire
unnatural to the end. We
cannot go to the ocean
—we are going home.

To be human you got
to try everything, the
dates, figs, the special
shoes preventing
tragedy. A little town
in Massachusetts uses
clouds to spell your name.
You are a miny miny person.

At a gas station we
stopped at, Mess, I realized
everything. Thoughts of
the throat like a sharp yellow
noise, it won't go away, you
were always sorry. Look at you
in the factory making sausages,
look at what you've done.

Stupid blanket, rose of lace,
apostrophes of nothing.
Quickness of the heart
show yourself living. Drive
away from talk-talk, away
from fright. A colonnade

of trees for memory I
speak at the difficult sky.

Water as a mouthful
wind as water's hair I
make horses whenever
I want to. Count me, I'll
stay. Darkness, the room
goes darker—to hear someone
talking themselves down
from a place called there.

A castle making trees toward
other nations, the telephone
brings forth that you have not
changed—people make plans
for the weekend. North of the
magistrate, there's a three
bedroom apartment, a
good neighborhood. Quite.

East of the battery mouth,
Vermont will never be
the same, gone cloudy
Vermont is the mountains.
Whatever it was that happened
back there must have really
stuck on her. I gave up in the
forest when we ran out of feet.

Each under our own small
lightning, the walls give us
back our mouths. The pictures
getting better over time, we
never had a place like this.
Sometimes I dive underneath

the mountains, say
things in ruined water.

A rubber band, he tried
Olympic records. Dear
1987, more cartwheels. We
had a lot of time—sisters in
the kitchen like fire. Even a
child I had the shape and heart
of a woman, my face a room
with an Argentine accent.

One two three four five six
thank you! However wrong
we jump for the woman
starting the record player.
I begin to weep across the
floor. Pink tights like
minutes. A pronouncement
toward mountains.

The road tends old, far back.
Before this there was a small
country, before that, family.
A mother and her pink belted
shirt, my father a constant
narration of history. Amazing at
family we were good at jokes. Why,
why can't we go down there.

Sweetness of a goat you
came back. Walking like a
synthesizer you were the
most special mantel. And I put
my lipstick up on you and
you said, how romantic, and

I said hold a second, I said
let me take your face a minute.

Hysteria as a garden, a house
the colors are beautiful. Lush
raining sneakers we wanted to
know things, to swim Hawaii,
to go in France, all of us still
beneath lightning. I so dislike
what you've done with the place
but of course I'll let you go.

Small house, belong to no one.
I could take you swimming
I could let you drive, but sitting
here might do us good, bring
about some new blue flowers. You
cannot like what all this looks like,
the time it takes to tell any story, a
stranger, a man disinterested.

And we loved, loved and
they knew, to the point of
knowing the weather. The
smallest voice fell into the
floor and there was earth
for all the cancer. Most dire
when they drove away you
said do you trust my ceiling.

Sure, at times, we do
what we don't want to but
you know it could be great
good things—hurry, there
aren't all the days. I'll tell you
the whole story but only if

I can have it back, rivers
cost money, guards watching.

There, again, trots gloom, a
hot commodity, the sound
of bodies sleeping over,
sound them falling down.
Some conferences are just
stranger than others, welcome
to that. Let your hair fall down
let it fall into the stove.

Trees to hold beautiful,
vivid mothers, lunch, that
bare memory of places
to get back to, I still
remember times, they
were beautiful, many
reasoned and lovely, actual
things, young lady, everything.

The meadow to sleep in like
green was the night, faces as
great things to hold. Walk
with me a minute, blue flower,
to find the brave moon on its
hill. The tower and a bench for
all what cold. Dear friend, what
it costs to say anything at night.

So we've discovered that clouds
are not coming—still we
drive better at night. I kept
breaking on you. The years
don't even turn into stories
they become something else,

a chart, a piece of paper, a mild
hysteria, hysteria a garden.

Body like the clouds we fielded.
Resting blankets, shown belief,
sound no anger, love and its
bright knees. To know a river
to be older in an instant. A
bridge for standing, a towel for
our face, I don't need you anymore,
Finito! (and I slam the door).

A LONG TIME AGO IN THE U.S.A.

This is going to start with clouds, darlings, because that's
where it does. The humility! The bravery! The fact that we're here
doing this. Screw anyone who doesn't feel something
up here, I cannot tell you what it looks like
because some things you just have to see.

Henry going to Anchorage. I felt for his mother when
she said good-bye, had trouble looking at him, I thought
to hug her, I mean I wanted to.

Henry, your face, what you said to yourself ruddy,
I couldn't hear but happy it made me, what you'll
do in Alaska. What will you do in Alaska. The wind
and the stars, what of them. Alaska, the roads, Alaska.
Henry goes, Henry Brown, a possible teenager.

I ride a bus and Henry is Alaska, that's why
he has two ears and one mouth.

The machine, I love my mother, thoughts felt
in the mountains, in cars in the mountains,
rain and after the rain, more rain still. To remember
darkness, I have a friend afraid of the afternoon,
what it does to our eyes. She doesn't like sock in her face.

For Henry, meat, fresh meat, fire, fresh fish and
we buy fish in Cape Cod from Alaska, "I don't think
this is good," there are spills, how everything makes out.

Vermont the small and manageable, managing well. You sleep here
because I sleep here and the country is broken between. The
business of ruining everything, with a helmet on I can do anything.

How to rig up sturdy paper plates for hot dog dinners.
I speak too fast, your mouth unchanged, open these
mountains, they don't talk so loud. He chooses
animals, he kills the animals, Henry eats Alaska
in Alaska and one day he meets a bear.

Henry finds the bear in the late afternoon,
says something to himself but I cannot hear him.

It is not difficult to be pleasant
you should try smiling.

The Browns eat dinner in early Wisconsin, Henry has been
gone six days. They have a meat and a vegetable, they say grace.

You can be in Wisconsin, you can be in Alaska, but these days
you can't be in both, it doesn't work that way.

Delight. Confusion. When you see the bear, Henry, act surprised.

As good a time as any to remind you to wash often, be good
to your hair darlings, it owes you nothing.

What but the beach and look beautiful, who but the fatties, that's who.

What way is that rain going, I can't tell. I should've come with
you, I should not have stayed home. Henry, you smell good like my sister.

Here it comes, the rain, let's go wrapped in tinfoil. Take off
your seatbelt when there's a choice to be had. Everyone, thunder,
last one to leave the beach is a fattie in a two-piece. Henry!
The safest place is the car.

He said the thunder cleaned up, I can feel it
under me, whales, and the seagulls out in the rain,
they know better. Some people look like assholes,
they just do. That is why he is Henry and you are you.

The bay the ocean the lake, a beautiful canoe,
even Henry finds a pay phone, Alaska.

Who thought to save children with wings, or that they could
swim in the first place? The birds. The birds, that's who.

A beautiful canoe for sale and expensive. High tide
as good for a swim. People get divorces, yes, and
so fancy. You are so my sister. The house the moment
I had to get out, go in the water. It could be
cold, but I would, Henry. He swims, there are lakes, Alaska.

A bird on the beach, he came to Cape Cod. High tide
at seven, that's when the blue hand is on the seven and
the green hand is on the twelve. Today was breakfast.
Vacation. Three syllables I want back.
Throw those earrings back into the sea.

The road painted, knapsack belongings, the
look of things plundered, you eat for your hair.

When discussing frivolities I mean I want to, and the
horses ride to town, provisions if one needs them, if the
house had had hay. Fuck if you count things, stilled
privacy, the kind sound wills, blink, wills you
slow. The embarrassment of knowing but trying
anyway, Henry a letter, Mrs. Brown reads a letter:
I'm keeping up with the pace of things, the food is
fine, went dancing with nice people, love your
son.

If only the animals elsewhere had houses, the
animals taken out, made better (how little you
knew back then) I said are you getting all of this, which
windows will I have to close.

As you hear me then, when we pass the bears, the bears,
not needing much love, August, then August again,
when we wade through the creek where the
doctor lives, will it fix us, will it let us stay.

Some boat too close to the shore
all we can do is whistle it gone,
digressions found at swimming,
refusing seaweed, the wranglers, Henry
has come to cheer. When being righteous,
when Henry ate a deer, late July, that
hungry month, we kept looking
we kept close to a warmth. Undeniable
accents as kill, sure, he says, and he talks
like he's tucking me in. Like nothing
in the morning we will be gods
and at five o'clock there is no
need—blue hand on the five, the
green hand on the twelve—all of us
promising to be still for a time.

That's why we have two ears and one mouth, my mother's
friend, a voice I say, I could never have seen my sister's will,
my untoward invitation. What to do, just take what you need
out of it, learn to build a fire all across the beach, Alaska and
the fire, Alaska again, Henry, the sound of you talking to
yourself, good Alaska has lapped the visit, the presumption
of people choosing capitals, come over Henry, the river rooms.

And when you wake up you shall have that bunk bed feeling:
helplessness, the smell of the sound of a door, fear
with the noise of a spring, of thumping. The sound made
when wood floors are painted, when a counselor threatens
when the counselor's sent home, when she was a bitch anyway.
We called her ugly bitch. Henry turn the fire louder
because I'm cold.

And Henry dropped down
a well in Alaska and the
water and the dark darkness
and even if he had a phone,
and to know someone who
says good-night, and how I
know his boots, a pay phone,
a pay phone enduring, in the
wilderness I stretch my legs.

When the fidgets of a young boy
hungry and those near him,
the apple in his suitcase, and
wronged in the woods, the woods
responsible, the animals carry him
home, they tuck him in disheveled.
Imagining greens, he comes to an
understanding of exits, a cement
taking over, a bay in the guise of
starting again, friendliness has
gone swimming.

Why Henry calls those who haven't
called him back, have I said yet that
his most beautiful face, especially, he
thinks California, he says sad parts will go,
he'll wake up one day have nothing
he will go.

When his heart broke he could
break a heart with spelling.
He remembered water, remembered
home. A parking lot, a wagon undone,
the merciless fear and bears, Henry
hears German and he hits it like flies.

The kind of walk we'd rather not
talk of, at a certain point, we either
have to move someplace more feasible,
or speak to each other in better English.

When the animals happened in 1922, you weren't here.
Let me tell you, this was not the countdown of bridges
this was something entirely. They thought I was
a nice person, they'd invite me to their homes and
let me bathe. They had in common prayer, we looked like
accommodations, said good-bye for love. In the most
careless states we take care of ourselves, the mountains,
magnificent parking lots full. The way you work how you do,
I hear grass, I want dirt, hear the sound of you and your river.

If after all of this you're still wondering, you must not have
listened to the bravery, the electric things I kept losing.

Because we're allowed to
look like that again, clapping
meadow of bright corners,
the man walking me into
myself, and there are times I want
to be fixed to something. Say what
you wish—I'm not a fighter,
I cannot keep up with the clouds,
brother gods divided into six
part waves. Stop looking that
way, pensive isn't good on you,
—I'm happy in my small
electric chair, lamp unknown to
the table, song home. The blank
river gods underwhelmed,
wondering who hurt who more.
Streets won't go away. The
small toothed calendar says
stop stalling. In trouble the facts,
their lack of response, try
holding on, you, brave, idiot
root of the maple tree.

And when the face changes,
blanket on the floor, an animal
happily clapping to the doors,
my house will be mine again.
Holy bodies figured indoors, we
woke ourselves, leaning into the forest,
we leaned into the room. There was
nothing we were, nothing and that
matters. Fly away little lie down, go
away from here; impatient weather
will break on you, bring you toward
insurance flowers. Anxious
window not saying a thing,
I don't know how to gauge defeat.
There are still more chances,
little friends, the way wind
would form a thing. I decided
to become wonderful, found my
legs and removed a heart.

That is the mind I am talking about.
That wind that fire that way of saying
something so unlike anything as familiar
as a hand, a hand on your body. My body
breaking the ocean in tiny moments of
excitement. Excitement like a chair, like
an idea in an evening, something not even
pretty, not even false. You are beside me,
Mountain, Face, you're like wallpaper,
swallowing kites. Nothing but nonsounds
in gone hollowed rooms. The rooms have been
closed forever, the rooms have been sad
forever. As with everything there are all
kinds of sadness and it comes to the
parties. You and all the parties. Your face
as a tiny machine, a tiny machine at night and so likely.
Like fog, the warning was strong and perceptible.
This thing to do in the country! Yellow yellow
house to go home to, excitement all over the ocean.
Responsibility like watching. (All these women
making lamps.) A bedroom. I miss loneliness and what it
causes, a moon that says LOOK, the moon the same

moon moaning itself, er, ak, it moves to tomorrow.
Everything is connected to the fault line in the rug, like
California came inside, like it needed to sit down,
broken. Everything not counting nothing, which
itself deserves praise. What I mean is farewell,
go on and do great things; the ocean today the ocean
all over the ocean is always the ocean, our faces.

COLOPHON

Bright Brave Phenomena was designed at Coffee House Press,
in the historic Grain Belt Brewery's Bottling House
near downtown Minneapolis. The text is set in Minion.

AUTHOR'S ACKNOWLEDGMENTS

Thanks to the editors of the following journals in which some of these poems made their first appearances: *20012, 6x6, Boston Review, Conduit, Cultural Society, Denver Quarterly, Forklift, Ohio, notnostrums, Octopus, Supermachine, Vanitas, We Are So Happy to Know Something,* and *Zoland Poetry.* Thanks to Diane Simard and the participants of *Call and Response.* Also, thank you to the Song Cave for publishing "Building Castles in Spain, Getting Married" as a chapbook in 2009.

Not even kidding, thank you: Dobby Gibson, Chris Fischbach, Geoffrey G. O'Brien. Also tremendously, thank you Janke, Matt Hart, Jeannie Hoag, Zach Barocas, Angela Zammarelli, Ben Polk, Ben Estes, Alan Felsenthal, Jane Gregory, Geoff Hilsabeck, and Mike Schorsch for helping me get to these poems here. Thank you Jim Galvin, Rod Smith, Cole Swenson, Connie Brothers, and thanks to my dear peers from the city of Iowa City for all the forms of support and for whenever there was dancing.

I am grateful to the Fund for Poetry.

Perpetual thanks to Chris (again), Jessica, Linda, Anitra, Tricia, Andrea, Tony, Kelsey, and Allan for the incredible work you do and for the fantastic community you create.

Dear Nay, Mike, Daniel, Sara, and Ollie. And to my sweet friends, thank you, a lot.

FUNDER ACKNOWLEDGMENT

Coffee House Press is an independent nonprofit literary publisher. Our books are made possible through the generous support of grants and gifts from many foundations, corporate giving programs, state and federal support, and through donations from individuals who believe in the transformational power of literature. Coffee House Press receives major operating support from the Bush Foundation, the Jerome Foundation, the McKnight Foundation, from Target, and in part by a grant provided by the Minnesota State Arts Board, through an appropriation by the Minnesota State Legislature from the Minnesota Arts and Cultural Heritage fund with money from the vote of the people of Minnesota on November 4, 2008, and a grant from the Wells Fargo Foundation of Minnesota. Coffee House also receives support from: three anonymous donors; Suzanne Allen; Elmer L. and Eleanor J. Andersen Foundation; Around Town Literary Media Guides; Patricia Beithon; Bill Berkson; the James L. and Nancy J. Bildner Foundation; the E. Thomas Binger and Rebecca Rand Fund of the Minneapolis Foundation; the Patrick and Aimee Butler Family Foundation; the Buuck Family Foundation; Ruth and Bruce Dayton; Dorsey & Whitney, LLP; Mary Ebert and Paul Stembler; Fredrikson & Byron, P.A.; Sally French; Jennifer Haugh; Anselm Hollo and Jane Dalrymple-Hollo; Jeffrey Hom; Carl and Heidi Horsch; Stephen and Isabel Keating; the Kenneth Koch Literary Estate; the Lenfestey Family Foundation; Ethan J. Litman; Carol and Aaron Mack; Mary McDermid; Sjur Midness and Briar Andresen; the Rehael Fund of the Minneapolis Foundation; Deborah Reynolds; Schwegman, Lundberg & Woessner, P.A.; John Sjoberg; David Smith; Kiki Smith; Mary Strand and Tom Fraser; Jeffrey Sugerman; Patricia Tilton; the Archie D. & Bertha H. Walker Foundation; Stu Wilson and Mel Barker; the Woessner Freeman Family Foundation; Margaret and Angus Wurtele; and many other generous individual donors.

ART WORKS.
arts.gov

MINNESOTA
STATE ARTS BOARD

TARGET

To you and our many readers across the country,
we send our thanks for your continuing support.

MISSION

The mission of Coffee House Press is to publish exciting, vital, and enduring authors of our time; to delight and inspire readers; to contribute to the cultural life of our community; and to enrich our literary heritage. By building on the best traditions of publishing and the book arts, we produce books that celebrate imagination, innovation in the craft of writing, and the many authentic voices of the American experience.

VISION

LITERATURE. We will promote literature as a vital art form, helping to redefine its role in contemporary life. We will publish authors whose groundbreaking work helps shape the direction of 21st-century literature.

WRITERS. We will foster the careers of our writers by making long-term commitments to their work, allowing them to take risks in form and content.

READERS. Readers of books we publish will experience new perspectives and an expanding intellectual landscape.

PUBLISHING. We will be leaders in developing a sustainable 21st-century model of independent literary publishing, pushing the boundaries of content, form, editing, audience development, and book technologies.

VALUES

Innovation and excellence in all activities

Diversity of people, ideas, and products

Advancing literary knowledge

Community through embracing many cultures

Ethical and highly professional management
and governance practices

Join us in our mission at coffeehousepress.org